Brain Works

Brain Works

Poems by Arthur Ginsberg

David Robert Books

© 2019 by Arthur Ginsberg

Published by David Robert Books
P.O. Box 541106
Cincinnati, OH 45254-1106

ISBN: 9781625493354

Poetry Editor: Kevin Walzer
Business Editor: Lori Jareo

Visit us on the web at www.davidrobertbooks.com

Acknowledgements

Earlier versions of these poems have appeared in the following journals:

Beyond Forgetting 2009: Pacific Sunset

Neurology: Consciousness

Connecticut River Review: Day on Fire

JAMA 1996: Bogdan Vuksanovich

At the Springtree Cafe: Stroke

Ashes Caught on the Edge of Light: Cruiser

Faith is the Next Breath: Paul Thek's *Warrior Leg*

The Comstock Review 2016: Conductor

Blood and Bone—Poems by Physicians: Bill of Lading

Neurology: Holy the Hand

Cloudbank 2009: Ode to Vision

Walking the Panther: Autopsy Poem

Georgetown Review 2005: Turning 60

The Anatomist: When the Earth Trembled

Argestes 2009: Sweetbriar

Floating Bridge Review: Crossing Over

Faith is the Next Breath: Faith

Faith is the Next Breath: Exhalation

Xanadu 2016: Polysyllabic

*For all my teachers and patients
who taught me reverence
for the human condition*

Table of Contents

Unpack a Brain................................13

Line Drive......................................14

Pacific Sunset................................16

Daisy, Daisy...................................18

Night Train Villanelle....................19

Consciousness...............................20

Day on Fire....................................21

The Journey..................................22

Bogdan Vuksanovich....................24

Stroke..26

Brain Work....................................27

Cruiser..28

On the Battlefield.........................30

Paul Thek's *Warrior Leg*...............31

Her Life was a Concerto...............32

Mincing Garlic..............................35

Rictus..36

Cirrhosis.......................................37

Plastination..................................39

The Butterfly Garden.....................41

Requiem for the Paleolithic Brain..43

Conductor......................................45

Solitude...46

Pica at Altitude.............................47

Bill of Lading................................48

Holy the Hand...............................50

Ode to Vision................................52

Autopsy Poem...............................54

Meditation at Esalen.....................56

Poseur...57

Labor Day 2016............................58

Santorini.......................................60

Whither Thou Goest......................61

Holy Flesh....................................62

At the Funeral..............................64

Dancing with Another..................65

Turning 60...................................67

Sound View.................................68

Now as Then..................................69

The Bones are Singing...................70

Nautilus...71

When the Earth Trembles..............73

Sweetbriar.....................................74

On a Perspective of Things............75

Polysyllabic...................................76

Crossing Over...............................77

Faith..79

Exhalation.....................................80

The Words 81

Inviolable......................................84

Unpack a Brain

Unpack a brain from its lock-box.
Roll it into a sheet like pastry dough
measuring 2.5 square feet. Ignore
the shrieks of severed relations, uncaged
baboons. Synapses sizzle and spark
like downed wires. Spread before you—

Olympus and Hiroshima.
Pick up the cookie cutter.

Choose which shape you prefer.

Line Drive

I had come from a dying man's room.
What I said spoke to the cancer
eroding his brain—how his right side
would become limp, he would slowly
slip into a coma. And I pointed out
the silver shadow on black film,
from the foot of his bed, staying
at bed's length from him and his widow-to-be.
Said too little, too quickly
for the quivering ears and lips
where death was digging in, and I forgot
to touch or be touched. Going home

I passed a schoolyard.
It was a fine day, the light scattered
in shafts on the dark brown earth
of the baseball diamond. Clover grew
in clumps by the side of the field,
their white tendrils pulling in the bees.
Everything was shouting, *hallelujah,
alive, alive!* A mother cat cuffed
her kittens into line, taught them
to balance on the schoolyard big toy,
old retreads hooked one to another,
swaying in the breeze. I vaulted the fence

to get closer to the game, when the batter
hit a line drive into the pitcher's stomach.
He dropped like a stone, but was in moments
surrounded by Billy and Peter and Rob,
the first baseman holding his head, his
sobbing, coaxing him to breathe, *you'll live,
it will be okay.* I knew then,

I must go back to the man dying
in white linen, and say nothing more
than the warmth of my hands on his.

Pacific Sunset

A rat's nest of tangles and plaques
chokes my mother's brain,
as she sits on Chesterman's Beach,
fiddling with her grey wig,
unaware of the egg-omelet stain
that batiks her blouse, and tell-tale
wet spot between her legs, oblivious
to the booming Pacific that stretches
before her befuddled eyes, the salmon-pink
sunset, I have brought her to see.

There's our house, son,
she says, pointing to a cloud,
and, *isn't Montreal beautiful?*
In the next breath, she berates me
for marrying a *shiksa,* then asks,
a moment later, if she has said
anything wrong. I cling for comfort
to the sough of beach wind through
stunted pines. *Reuben,* (my father,
gone ten years) *I want to go home,
now,* she whines, a bewildered smirk
on her face. *Sure Ma,* I reply, and I take
her arm, light as a bird bone,
steer her back to the cabin I have rented.

By candlelight, I spoon into her mouth,
mammaliga, the corn gruel she loves
from Pietra Namsk in Romania,
where she grew up. What tenderness
I hold for this marred mind, how fine
to have known this palace of her spirit,
the template for mine. Lip smacking
speaks to a wordless content,
as she sundowns with the light,

leaves me holding
an empty bowl in the dark.

Daisy, Daisy

Thrown on the slag heap, each one
bears the stamp of metal. Simply
to have come this far merits praise.
For the visitor, there is John Charles,
example of gleaming chrome in opaque
corneas that see in the dark. He steers
by the soft crunch of hardwood floors
with a touch of divine carburetion.
Other fenders are broken by accident
and time, scattered on Lazy-Boy re-
cliners. With a Bentley's elegance,
John Charles glides through a doorway
to the terminal chassis of my mother.
He caresses withered hands, implores
in a falsetto voice, *Won't you sing
with me? Won't you sing? Daisy,
Daisy, give me your answer true......*
Behind wreckage, she flickers, headlamps
briefly brilliant, she finishes with him,
on a bicycle built for two. And
there is a shining of all the fenders.

Night Train Villanelle

Engineer, take Mother gently down the track.
A solid oak casket holds my priestess in white.
Soul, seek comfort beyond the watchman's shack.

Of sorrow, she would say, this world does not lack.
Compassion ruled her heart with a warrior's might.
Engineer, help Mother gently down the track.

Here's a handful of earth to marry heaven back,
David's amulet on her chest glows against the night.
Soul, gather comfort beyond the watchman's shack.

Bones bereft of breath grow light until they crack.
You were summer lilacs with a bit of garlic bite.
Engineer, ease Mother gently down the track.

Yis-g'dal, v'yis-g'dash, cover me with ash and sack.
How should a stockyard mourner anticipate such blight?
Soul, find comfort beyond the watchman's shack.

Death comes surely, as no birth would turn day black.
Closed eyes harbor peace without motive to indict.
Mother, round-trip is the ticket, throw my luggage on the rack.
Soul, seek comfort beyond the watchman's shack.

Consciousness

floats in the delicate
                    ether of butterflies,
brain spilt
                    into itself, warbling
through a garden of grey matter,
                    an unmistakable
interiority that does not emote,
                    gabble or quack,
is pre-syntax and babble,
                    reigns like a cloud
over the birth of flowers,
                    gazes across a moat
into the forest
                    of pheromones and photons,
the din of decibels,
                    and into the reservoir
of itself; a pool
                    of unshattered meniscus,
untouched by the tongue
                    that comes out of the mouth,
flicking the surface
                    like trout. Mind sifts
the pre-syllabic library
                    in every ridge and rut,
lifts on muslin wings
                    beyond the circuitry,
and waits for the anesthesia
                    of sleep, when consciousness
fibrillates, set free
                    to orbit in the galaxy
of Galileo's imagery.
                    Without it, worlds that men propose,
reality or dream,
                    would be unmindfully comatose.

Day on Fire

He started the day like a match struck against a rough surface,
the tip, tungsten brilliant, laced with crimson and magenta.
Ingots of light poured through the windshield. Then the slow
drift of flame down the scrawny stem, leaving behind
its charred resume. Who can believe things burned away,
ever return? Music poured like smoke out of the speakers,
the speed limit was 60, to match the bowing of the cello
in Bach's third suite. Arachnid fingers amplifying the vibrato,
horse hair spilling wave after wave into the varnished grain
of its body. You could hear the genius in the last movement
galloping like a herd of wildebeests going over a cliff.
Gouts of dissonance coming out of nowhere—the sheer immensity
of an extraordinary brain rollicking through wildflowers.
A fifth wheel passed him, belching exhaust, hybrids ganged up
on him like hornets, approaching the toll booth. My god! It felt good
to let go, to be out of control in a flurry of sunspots glinting
like rhinestones or a runway's lights, down the ribbon of Bots Dots.
He began to cry for the other drivers imprisoned in their cocoons, stared
aghast at the woman in a glass booth who asked him for five dollars.
This is the journey ascending to the divine with grappling hooks
on your ankles and a garrote around your throat. The day on fire, no
speed limit, and the water cannons aimed and ready. The green Go light
winked him past the turnstile, Bach evaporated from the speakers,
he could smell the road stink enveloping him, familiarity of routine—
some cop in ambush, clocking speed, and the sky too blue and imperfect,
flaunting crows and a few smudged clouds. Heaven's gates closing. Now
the air conditioner filled his ears with the white noise of wheezing angels,
as if to say, this never happened. How can we know what moments are real,
what imagined, consumed like the matchstick? But a tiny part of him knew
he would hold on to the engine's rhythm of hope and faith. All the way
down the road to the empty parking lot at the end of the pavement.

The Journey

My first day on the wards,
the senior resident handed me a white coat
emblazoned with the twin serpents of Asclepius,
and a stethoscope, I proudly draped around my neck.
I thought I knew everything
about the dying patient assigned to me.

I listened studiously to John Doe's lungs
filling rhythmically from a little machine
with a red diaphragm that pumped up and down
and made a hissing sound that reminded me
of the snakes embroidered on my collar.
I grew to know him over weeks,
to speak in code through a system of lid blinks—
the only muscles intact after a brainstem stroke.

White moth print of a wedding ring told me
he had loved, *Semper Fidelis* tattooed on his arm
honored his life as a warrior. Dropped suddenly
in the street, brought in by **911**. He had no family.
For days he stared like a walleyed pike
at perforated ceiling tiles—locked in—
the key forever lost on the riverbed.

I value lungs, that exquisite collection of air sacs
translucent as squid eggs, that endow our blood
with oxygen. My own lungs diseased from birth,
plagued by asthmatic wheeze, that once dropped me
like a stone, rounding second base after hitting
a home run—I recount this because of that day

when he signaled with three eye-blinks
that he wanted to fly. I tell you this because
I was asked to play God—
to cut him loose without a map or ladder

to climb back, to stop his lungs forever.
I tell you this to confess how my finger trembled
on the respirator switch. I knew then,
that I knew nothing.

I still remember the ache in my ribs,
how he searched my eyes, how he forgave me.

Bogdan Vuksanovich

At Interlaken, I push off on skates,
a rhythmic glissando across
the water's frozen face. Wind
works the high branches of the birches,
singing for sap's return. Earlier today,

I wore my instructor's cap, watched
Vuksanovich lurch from his wheelchair,
weave on sailor's legs to the table.
Medical students gawked at him;
a zoologic exhibit, *oohed* and *aahed,*
when I demonstrated damage according
to the textbook: eyes that ricocheted
like bullets, and ankles that pumped
like a startled deer at the stroke
of a reflex hammer. Signs of assault

on flowering brain, petals stripped
off matrix of tectum, tegmentum and pons,
weevils punching holes in hippocampus
and corpus callosum. I reveled
in this showpiece of pathology,
pulled out a slick word for impaired
coordination: *dysdiadochokinesia.*
They imbibed with zeal, pelted questions
like hardballs at a catcher. One student
blurted out, *can he get an erection?*
We were shamed. Bogdan retrieved a photo
of his year-old daughter. We admired
shining cheeks and tiny puckered lips.

By the boathouse, ice is cracked
and heaved, a tented jigsaw,
defiling geometry. What is broken
by nature is beautiful, creaks and groans
like human disease. I balance on one foot,
aware a slip could fracture bones.

Stroke

comes down, white as an avalanche,
erasing the playground of speech,
piles up in a drift at the tip
of Veida's tongue. She cannot repeat,
no ifs, ands, or buts, calls a comb,
bone, pen, *cow.* Frustration bleeds
through her brokenness, shudders in
chaotic clutching of spindly fingers,
as if, the right word could be plucked
from air. *Veida, Veida, listen to me.*
Follow my hand with your eyes. Eyes
brimming, she nods and follows, pendulum
on command. Stroke pitches camp,

lays rebar, pours cement. She grows to
know me and I, her, without ancestral
gift— small patch of brain, ordered as
the stars. From bedside, touch speaks,
vision flows in syllables, unfettered as
a child skipping rope. Fingertips vibrate
loquaciously as lips, extolling all the hope
of eighty-five years— married to darling Jack,
librarian, re-building spines of orphaned books.

Stroke binds her in the vault of our audacious
builder, pitiless as, buried alive. I visit Veida
each day, stunned by peals of laughter
at her own infirmity, that come from cosmic space,
roiling up through ghostly cracks to pry open,
the lock. Waylaid by walls, eyes fade,
no word to frame, *good-bye.*
Undoing speaks to the marvel of design—
more eloquent than speech, the vespers of silence.

Brain Work

This day please be calm.
Remember the winds blow as they will—
you are as a twig meant to bend
or crack. Outside the swords are drawn,
inside there is only your network's
muted thrum on this Sunday afternoon.
You must ask the right hemisphere
to dance with the left; a pas-de-deux
without thrust or flourish. You have seen
spittle flung from bellicose crowds,
slogans that ignore lessons gleaned
from the dead. Take a full moment
to honor your nose with the perfume
of Daphne that blooms by your door.
Return to the moment you watched
snowbirds fly into a perfect firmament.
Remember the first time we locked eyes,
giddy as children in the clover fields
of Dingle. Be calm this day,
lifted away on the wind chime's notes,
the tide that knows only to come and go.

Cruiser

    Sunday afternoon
on the back porch
      with a salmon sky
    and black waves rolling in;
        I want to board

      that slick blue cruiser
gliding past my window
    in white mist,
      feel the throb of her big engines
churn the water like a giant Mixmaster,
    share the froth foaming in her teeth.

Ample beyond
    the Lord Nelson cut of her prow,
low-slung in the back
      and all teaked-out on deck
with a slim stack billowing black
          into the sky.

From my porch
    I can see row boaters
envy-green as she slips by
      majestic as a whale,
      with the pilot spanky
in hand-stitched linen and gold-braided cap,
    bilges spouting like blowholes.

I imagine the CEOs down below,
    their women pimped out in designer jeans
pelting down martinis and beluga
    in a swell of New-Age piano.
    With each bow thrust and slick maneuver,
my mind sets sail and I know

       the deckhands who hunker down
            live inside of me,
                  small boys reckoning,
    lost at sea. I want to go aboard
before she vanishes
                behind the silvered poplars,

stand at her gimbaled stove,
   soufflés simmering in a pan,
act the suave man
        I am not,

visored yachtsman
      immune to the world's woes,
gin-fizz in hand with a swizzle stick,
      chit-chatting about races and cups,
   Noble-Tek software and runners-up.

   I pray to a faceless God
to let me live deep
      within the sanctuary of her keel;
the sort of bargain an atheist makes:
    one foot on the dock,
         one on the deck.

On the Battlefield

Mr. Carlisle beams a radiant smile,
tugs on the visored Marine Corps cap,
and tells me, *you're a good man.* Unaware
his memory has gone AWOL. He is back
on patrol in the highlands, with a finger
to his lips, eyelids twitching with each
staccato machine-gun burst, while
his daughter sits weeping in the chair
next to him. I move cautiously
through the tests because they are all
I have to make sense of this battle; X-ray blips,
risky genes hiding on chromosomes—signs
of a breach in the brain's sacristy. My grip
on reality weakens, and for a moment
I am crawling through a psychotic swamp,
time and space where I have never been,
entry denied. Saliva in my constricted throat
chokes me back into caregiver role, for surely
these people need something from me. *Just
keep dad happy,* his daughter implores.
I am happy, retorts Mr. Carlisle, as he stands
abruptly, gazing through his wife, Elizabeth.
Elbow cocked, fingers splayed rigidly,
vibrating at his brow. *Well done Sargent,*
he says. *Mess bell rang. It's time for chow.*

Paul Thek's *Warrior Leg*

Hirschorn Museum of Modern Art

Hacked off at the knee,
the calf of wood, wax, metal
and paint, sheathed by a leather thong,
glows with all its toes
in a Lucite reliquary. Weeps
for an unknown Roman soldier,
long gone, for the price paid

for an upright legacy,
its spouting artery
and shredded nerve. Once,
this was attached to a man
with a full set of bones,
who skipped and ran
and wrapped his legs
around a lover. Even now,

the artist's mind
lives in the shin's rosy shine,
as if he had been there
to catch the limb as it fell
from its thigh onto the blood-drenched
plain. Sad, disembodied leg,
you whisper from this jail,
splay your toes with plastic nails against
the unconsoling light.

Insensate, now, the band plays on
to sate the bellicose throng,
for those boys who fought after Troy,
who can no longer march.
Their epaulettes still stiff with starch,
and stumps like meat slabbed to the bone.

Her Life was a Concerto

in memory of
Jacqueline Dupres

Pizzicato

The sound is in the varnish, says the teacher,
laying the ancient cello at her feet.
He is a breathing thing with a slender neck,
strings, tightly strung across a resonant chest,
the high sheen of his skin reflecting back
to her, a freckled brow and glacial eyes.

For those tender years, he is the joy
between her legs, attentive to every pluck
and stroke, her lips curved as the scroll
which shapes his head, where tightening
controls the thickness in his voice.

She does not mind that he stands like a heron,
on one leg. With time, her fingers learn to fly,
deftly as a skylark, to press his tender vocal cords,
feel them press back, to make him come
in a tumult of notes, then, a little *pizzicato,*
as if to say, *let us frolic for awhile in the daffodils.*

*

Fortissimo

But for all his sonority, there is not enough
to fill her, so she fucks her sister's husband,
taking him in rapaciously, reaching around
to measure the distance between hard knobs
of his spine. Sweet sister Hillary; they
grew entwined as Siamese twins, one spirit
running down the beach, warmed one another
on cold nights and brushed each other's hair.

The man who weds his keyboard to her cello
cannot appease her soul that has already flown
and entered into the cello body like a sinner come
unto Christ, and taken into the grain of his wood.
London, New York, Madrid, Rome:

She's playing Elgar's concerto. Where the notes soar
to touch the cheek of heaven, on the topmost rung,
where her fingers are pressed high on his neck,
suddenly, she's wet. An outrageous puddle on the floor,
the bow launched from her hand, *fortissimo,* as if God,
in a fit of pique, had stripped His own goodness.

*

Pianissimo

Now, fingers become tortoise-slow
across the universe of his neck.
Wheel-chair bound, blind and deaf, she puts
her lover on the balcony, to die. His varnish
cracks and peels on a rain-swept night. In the end,
a brutal thievery assaults her brain, each sacred cell
gagged down to *pianissimo,* then struck away.
In the end, Hillary cradles Jacqueline's pain,
the empty hull of her body. She has flown to Elgar,
to Mozart, the heaven, she has given.

We are robbed and to God, what can we say?

Mincing Garlic

As I watch my friend wither day by day—
the small bulbs in his spinal cord
winking off one by one, like village lights
on a winter night viewed from a railroad track,
as I watch him slump in his wheelchair,
shackled by lifeless limbs and torso,
he speaks in a quiet voice—mostly gone
and losing ground each month. Two years
until an iron lung. He would like to deny
ripples on a pond that foreshadow
the gathering storm, makes light banter—
rage masked by the albatross of levity,
this betrayal of the flesh a lesson in futility.

Sleet whitens the windowpanes like ghosts
hovering over his head, the larch outside
has shed its needles onto the deck, carp
hide from coyotes at the bottom of the pond.
We mortals cannot reconcile the terminus,
pocket life like a round trip ticket.

May he navigate these rapids, peaceful
as slack tide, catch the wind for however long
he needs to ride. If anyone on high is listening,
to hell with you and your malevolent minions.

Grip still strong, my friend minces garlic
for a salad dressing, listens to the deluge
outside, clear-eyed and recalcitrant. Breath
insistent as branches that scrape the wall.

Rictus

The men in white coats call it, *rictus*—
the death mask smile. They say
just a spasm of the risorius muscle,
but who knows what that grin really means?

Last night beneath a gibbous moon,
a cougar killed a deer on the lawn. Stripped
the muscle off its right haunch, strewed
intestines coiled like springs on the grass,
deflated lungs straddling the windpipe, but
her lips curled in a most beatific smile.

I remember the agony on my father's face
as cancer tore through his body,
and blood spilled onto the hospice floor.
Then, the letting go, his jaw unclenching
like a clamshell, into a prophetic smile.
Rictus, the nurse said, patting my shoulder—
just a reflex of the dead—but I imagine

he may have seen something we cannot know—
perhaps an image of my mother haloed
in sunlight, leaning against a birch tree, holding
her white terrier, Teddy. And he knew
he had found what lucky men find in this life.

Now, when I meditate, those sweet souls
shimmer before me in a radiant light, just
out of reach. Something, even a deer sees—
this other place, this infinity beyond
the savage night, that summons the last smile.

Cirrhosis

*Think of a palm tree growing out of your navel,
also known as the Caput Medusae,* says the professor,

*named after the monster who had hair
made out of snakes according to Greek mythology,*

placing her stethoscope over the swollen veins,
so her brood of students can listen to

the Cruveiler-Baumgartner murmur, a sign
of increased pressure and blood flow in the liver.

Sweating under my white coat I palpate
with my fingertips, the cirrhotic edge of a ruined organ

that seesaws beneath this man's twelfth rib
with each inhalation. Imagine this human being,

eyes wide with fear as stethoscope after
stethoscope with cold diaphragms interrogate

his belly-button, their reaction punctuated by
oohs & aahs, while the professor in stentorious voice

warns of impending catastrophic hemorrhage!
Did anyone ask the man his name?

We move on to the next bed and the next,
following and clucking devoutly after the mother hen

pecking her way through this labyrinthine ward
of agonal Brooklyn souls, delirious and hallucinating,

hoisted on their own alcoholic petards, some blinded
by aftershave lotion cut with wood methanol.

By midnight I begin to understand the meaning
of misery, the tawny color of livers

depicted in textbooks, the jaundiced hue
of bilirubin-tinged eyes. By midnight,

I come 'round to John Doe, hold his hand,
ask his name, the whereabouts of his children

and wife. This, before he suddenly gurgles,
clutches his throat and spits a stream of blood that hits me

like a geyser in the chest—then he is gone.
I stumble to the dorm, thirsty for what might kill me.

Plastination

Start with a corpse, the bluish
      monogram of *livedo reticularis*
   on its flanks. A whiff
of plastic polymer and formalin
      in the air. A little man
   wearing a black fedora
and the hieroglyphs of grandiosity
      cut into his cheeks,
   who promises to resurrect
your lover's body, pristine
      as Amenhotep,
   for a thousand years.
Vacuum the fluids and fat, force feed
      the arteries, like a goose
   for *foie gras*, with rubber that glows
like neon. Pack the muscles with silicon,
      inflate
   the blanched nipples. Bisect
the skull to reveal her brain—
      a pasha perched
   in the minaret of his caliphate—
its ruts and ridges
      glossy now,
   crisscrossed by veins,
as if, the love she lavished
      on you, was still
   contained. That little man
will slice thin sections
      of her heart, like ham
   on a butcher's blade;
a painting framed
      to hang in your mausoleum.
   Walk between the stainless steel
vats and jars on shelves,
      filled with bright remains

from someone's gutted husk.
Ask yourself if Mozart's music
    could be any sweeter,
had we, his pauper's body
to gawk at, in a glass case. Ask
    the man in the black fedora,
why he seeks immortality,
what blinded him, in the body's geometry,
    to the weightlessness of dust.

The Butterfly Garden

> Like the entomologist in search of
> brightly colored butterflies, my
> attention hunted, in the garden
> of gray matter, cells with delicate
> and elegant forms, the mysterious
> butterflies of the soul.
>
> Santiago Ramon Y Cajal

If not for Lord Brain,
who could have imagined

the nature of a thought
spun in its labyrinth

of Cajal's filigree. More
lustrous than silver,

and wily as a trout,
silent to the surface

before it's caught. Or re-
entry deep into the circuitry

where neurons that fire
together, wire together,

and etch their signature
in the hall of memory,

selected by linguistics
our predecessors taught.

And when, like petals,
thoughts unfold

and drop onto the lips, become
speech, become song, or

motoric offerings, 2 million years
of artistry murmur in the wings.

Requiem for the Paleolithic Brain

Let me cauterize
        with the surgical wand,
        that limbic almond named, *amygdala,*

a brimstone repository
        nestled deep in the brain's putty—
        sulphurous nugget

of Neanderthal rage
        like a saber-toothed tiger
            fecklessly seeded by creation

inside our heads—
        once I believed
        that Sapiens was divine,

hairless inheritors
        fashioned from the sacred dust
        of whirling galaxies,

now weary
        in our monstrous fits and starts
        through clotted millennia,

castaways
        in the two-by-two ark, disguised
        in a thin mantle

of gray matter—
        how evolution's gamble has hurt
            our lives, spilled this unsavory rage

in fiery cages
        where smoke snakes into nostrils
        leaving blackened lungs

hungry for air
         in a cave of lengthening shadows,
         bat guano and silence.

We were hobbled
         in the steaming kitchen
         before we chimped across the savannahs,

delusional,
         we were in control
         of this vestigial bomb that ticks

inside an unholy spirit—
         tick, tick, tick... into an opaque
         dawn of spliced chromosomes

annealed to steel fists.

Conductor

Once, I wanted to be a conductor like Klemperer,
baton raised like a lightning rod awaiting the divine strike,
to be swept away on a tide of gut and varnished wood
and shiny metals, embouchures feeding my ears, my mind
with celestial thunderstorms, cymbals, voices from deep space,
the hiss of snakes snared on the drums. Sometimes one knows
what direction to take—neon signs flashing, sky vault wide
open over the vast meadow of possibility, the rightness of
marrow throb. Yet, I played deaf, went out on the icy streets
of Montreal for another game of hockey, with the strains of
Mahler clinging to my skates. I can still be that boy now,
banging out arpeggios until my fingertips swelled. My teacher
who bribed me with baklava and milk, watched my spark fizzle
in a whirlpool of distractions. Stethoscope trumped baton
in the halls of Hippocrates. I conducted Brahms behind the wheel,
down the glazed avenues of winter, on the wards of the addicted
and afflicted, at altitude on the flanks of Kilimanjaro. All this
music that Klemperer unleashed, notwithstanding paralysis
that left him wheel-chair bound before his beloved orchestra.
Memory throbs like a hangover, this ember that smolders
like his gaze through horn-rimmed glasses. Now, in middle age,
I eat oysters. I drink gin and tonic. The terror of so many notes
shackled to the right half of my brain, humming to themselves
like mad men, striving to cross the great divide into words.
A multitude of God songs streaming like electrons through silver,
amped up by the echo chamber of my skull. My last chance
fading on arthritic knees, pianissimos, notes opaque as cataracts.
Small boy on the podium awash in an ocean of encores and bravos.
Sometimes at dusk, in the stillness of groves when Arbutus trunks
are laved with gold, I can say I am a conductor, no one to refute it.
The music in a circuit board soldered to my soul. I can remember
the ancient melody played out in the rhythm of our limbs as we ran
through the untrammeled world beneath jeweled heavens, before
some men gathered the music, ignited it like comets in their hands.

Solitude

The snow blows all night,
covering the earth's gash, white nettles
on the tongue, salt in the eyes.
I huddle in the shift of love's
black ice, last year's calendar
undone under drifts. Solitude measured
by inches on the rail.

I turn into myself,
away from sleet's lash,
mesmerized by the haloed lilac
at the end of the street, each bough
shrouded in the flurry, footprints
erased by fiction.
The absence of me louder
than silence of snow.

This white chrysalis is my paradise
lost like crystals on a windshield,
a memory of my seventh year, when
I packed a valise and left my house
in a snowstorm, dug a cave and lay down
to sleep. Alone then as I am now,
waiting for my father to carry me home.

Pica at Altitude

Coming into camp,
crackers smeared with Vegemite,
tinned sardines. The American doctor
grinds their soft spines between his teeth.
Ravenous for fish at altitude. Oil
to the cheekbones and his lips tingling.
After each climb, he hustles down
boulder-strewn trails, makes a beeline
for the afternoon buffet. The sherpas
hunched over lentils, watch with dismay.

At dusk he dips his battered life
into the Dudh Kosi's roiling waters,
numbs the scourge of sickness
in hypothermia. By Lhotse and Everest,
solitude blooms in his bones, turns him
to his face. When the Blue Bharal sheep
scatter to drink, he watches from a ridge
beneath a blessing of snowbirds.

Appetite sated, so opened up
by the unbearable terror of bliss,
he petitions the summit, *burn me, bury me*
like Breitenbach under your skin, coward
that I am. Retreats into the small parameters
of the sleeping bag, shields his head.

Bill of Lading

Anton Steiner sits behind a rosewood desk
in the ivory tower across the street from
Armageddon. I stand before him, buck private
intern, drenched in sweat and grime. After
48 hours of emergency duty, he demands
a bill of lading; handwritten cards on seventy
Brooklyn souls in various stages of entropy.

I want to say I am fatigued and my feet ache, that
I don't give a damn for documentation, that
I want to sleep and shower, the way he did
before work. I want to say, the cards will not tell
Jose Martinez's story, how he died in my arms,
a chunk of steak wedged in his windpipe.

He is as impassive as dust, the metal
of his eyes, a glacial blue. He has forgotten
the feel of membranes, slick in a split-open chest,
putrefaction from an addict's abscess, the **all clear**
shout before paddles convulse an arrested heart.

The cards will not recall Dora, bag-lady from Flatbush,
who thinks I am her reincarnated son from Jerusalem,
will not recapture one iota of my pleasure when
I cut through Amber's pantyhose, to reveal
the glistening head of her newborn son. Or horror
of a man who penetrated himself with a lightbulb,
forgetting glass is fragile. I want to tell Steiner

that these cards are old news, the ink was spilled
hours ago, that the ink ran like blood to my knees
and elbows, that the world is strangling in ink
and paper, that neon patterns on oscilloscopes
are something we have invented to detach us
from matters of the heart. In mellifluous voice,

he asserts, *the report is due by nine, your future depends on it, that is all.*

Holy the Hand

    in bird-bone digits,
perched on lunate pedestal,
    sheathed in the rosy glow
of cuticles and skin.
    Each finger tethered by tendon
can curl to beckon,
    go straight to castigate.
Tight as mortise and tenon,
    a benediction
of rack and pinioned knuckles,
    exquisite pinch of pulp,
square taste of fist. Holy the fingers

    splayed in flow and form,
the Pieta's palms upturned
    to pray, and manifold
in all the ways of caress,
    punch and slap. Nuanced
on piano keys, with the sensitivity
    of an armadillo's snout,
some clenched, others outstretched
    as Michelangelo's. Holy the hand

in profligate freedoms,
    dextrous bequest
of our mathematician.
    Like a macaw's beak, tenacious
as its talons, mercurial as mimosa.
    Prehensile in grasp,
the messenger of intention, and when
    sight fails, becomes the eyes…

Holy the plastic surgeon,
    master of tendon and bone,
who rescues the shredded hand

   from a grinder intended for corn,
and like the Eucharist,
     consecrates a new finger and thumb,
strong enough to grasp a wrench,
     turn a bolt till this man's job is done.

Ode to Vision

Give way to the mechanic
who ratchets eye-lids up like a drawbridge
across the skull's dry sockets,

the glazier who fires the frit
into smooth discs of magnification,
suspended by caliper, like a moonstone
in the vault of each iris. Because the eyes

are an umbilicus to the world,
tether us to the names we've learned
to call heaven and earth, oak and fire,
know then the parallax of vision's garden
and all its plenty:
        the bee, the Bob-O-Link
        and Hop Hornbeam,
        the Lammergeyer,
that magisterial bird coasting the edge
of your perimeter. Let nothing blind

the millimeter pinholes of your pupils,
as you peer into the gloaming
of a day drawn down to rest;
        a rowboat bobbing at dusk,
        the shining lemon of owls' eyes
blazing in the forest. Invite the astronomer

to marry light to your eyes,
and amplify the star-crossed rays
from the latitudes of gaze, to meet
midway behind the ophthalmic globes, there,
to explode in a caravan of imagery
that drifts upstream into the river-
bend's soft folds where the oarsman off-loads
its cargo into your seams. Take heart

in Hyperion who hurls lumens
across the cosmic meadow, unveiling
Eos, goddess of dawn beneath the moon-
lapped shadows, crowned by swallows.
Sight comes with the brush
of pale fingers on feathered lash,
life's first and last epiphany poured
through the waterfall of your eyes.

Autopsy Poem

I knew your eyes,
shining, carnivorous,
irises like Van Gogh's blue.
Lips supple as a willow bow.
Such ruddy flesh.

I stand by the mortician and stare
at death's violaceous rigor.
Was it you, that purple thigh,
puckered breasts and talcum mask,
dumb bas-relief in last repose?
He slits and cuts you to the quick,

decapitates the skull, scoops away
the brain. Intestines ripple
in a bowl as your last meal
is milked out like the stuffing
of a sausage. Ovaries harvested
like walnuts, blueprints
plundered for eternity.

Last to leave is the heart, ripped
from its vine with a whimper of blood,
dying gently in the sink.
I remember how it tendered my ribs,
invited my chest to takes its measure,
counted the time like a metronome
saying that every clock winds down.

When the knife is set aside,
the organs catalogued and stored,
a stripped chassis is all that remains.

Your soul never surrendered here,
never passed through the butcher's hands.
It flies beyond the morgue's dark door.

Meditation at Esalen

Something about a squadron of pelicans at dawn.
The fog burned off, horizon unlouvered,
the leaders out in front, skirting the sandstone cliffs.
A loose chevron of birds effortless on invisible currents,
the translucent velum of their gullets, ladles
crisscrossed by capillaries, bulging with mackerel.

We don't know why they go wingtip-to-tip
like the Blue Angels, who orchestrates their ranks
or the signals given, if their general is arrogant
as Napoleon or bound by the bonds of fealty, flying

over salt-laced spume to the sea lions' barking tunes.
We don't know how their ancestor, Archaeopteryx,
half bird, half lizard, crawled out of the swarming kitchen,
to witness the birth of flowers, and lifted into air.

I stare at them from my armchair on the cliff
until they dwindle into small specks, close my eyes
and fly above the ragged edge of earth, above
thunderheads scudding in from the west. For a moment
I ride the updraft of their wings with perfect clarity,
one slow breath after another. Legend has it,

pelicans lose their vision after crash-diving into the sea.
So many ways to go blind. My mind jostled by intrusions.
Beautiful, the way kelp beds sway and unfurl far below.

Poseur

What am I behind this medical mask
but a poseur two feet distant measured
by tubes of the stethoscope from any heart
scarecrow in a waistcoat
on the battlefield's bully pulpit spreading
my vital lie of character like crows
running off at their beaks blind
to light climbing the poplars
intricacy of wheat bending in the breeze
geometry of disease like cracked ice
up in tents of hard harmonics
what is to become of me without
a face the masquerade unhinged from feathered
headdress and papier-mâché cheeks
a voyeur at best of human misery
I tried when you stared into my eyes and saw
what has strangled all these tortuous lines
to be what I could not become

Labor Day 2016

Let the clay, like every other day,
spin on its wheel with its wet imprint

of gray fingers. Let trains rumble through
dusk's blue light, towing Pullman cars

into the night, designed by the man who began
the fight against labor's injurious legacy.

Consider children hobbled at the knee, mere
shadows in dust motes, squeezed to an anemic

marrow, and eyes gone dark as a starless night,
blind as man's unbridled greed. From holy hands

unwound the coolies' toil, torn from
their turmeric and tea, the endless steel

rails snaking across forest and ravine.
For the picket men and the sit-in men

let the rapturous clay spin itself bone-dry—
all that we shape and fire in the kiln

breaks back into sand stripped clean
by nature's tempestuous sea—we cannot

shape time's hydraulic crush nor boast
a rain-bowed glaze that does not fade. Gaze

upon the lumberman's, longshoreman's toil,
their purple bruise of torn sinew and muscle,

my father's face gaunt as the workman he sculpted,
his youth spent as a soldier when world war erupted.

Never forget when the trains rumble through,
the welcome that read, *Arbeit Macht Frei.*

Now return from the picnics and the parades,
work's history eclipsed in a flight of balloons.

Get back to the shapeless lump on the wheel—
days of our years colored by the pottery we make.

Santorini

for Jack Gilbert

The slate path winding through
lava rocks, small dogs sprawled
in the sun, a flare of white-washed villas,
lemon and peach pastels.
The old woman wrapped in black.

I climb farther to where the path blends
into a donkey track strewn with pumice
between the twisty honey locusts.
I've come here for Hippocrates's cure:
oil to the cheekbones,
slabs of Manouri cheese, sweet cherry tomatoes.
I've come here empty to walk these stones,
to sift the soil this island birthed
from a power coiled miles beneath my feet.

But the earth stays silent, holding its rhythms,
wind strumming through olive groves.
Far below, the Blue Star ferry glides across
the caldera, Pyrgos and Monolithos,
shimmering wet light on distant hilltops.

I wander to the cliff's edge.
Windmill sails turn listlessly in the breeze.
Close my eyes and listen for the whispers
of Minoan voices after their world shattered.

If I must go this way,
let it be to the lap of waves against a hull,
the staccato of olives striking the ground,
every day a flask of oil poured
from one night into another.

Whither Thou Goest

What I fear most now
grown older than I ever hoped to be
is the glue on my shoes
that binds me to the hill in Peru
where I traveled up scree
groin-pulled boot-strapped through hanging moss
through seventeen species of hummingbirds
a blind crow blundering through stalks of corn
coveting the condor on his throne
I did not know how small my child
I did not know what questions or even the path
back pack of the sick wards strapped to me
like a sea anchor in tow
and Ruth's *whither thou goest I will go*
saying no in my head
lost in the riverbed's moan
all my teachers dead their sweet
wise faces in the snow of this mountain saying
you are ready now
to learn before you go

Holy Flesh

After a life in pursuit of youth's fountain,
after the quest for immortality,
we need to see through
the papery-thin skin of our beloved partners,
to hold the slow honey of ripe at the end
of yearning, while sex raps its knuckles
on the sliding door,
while the train pulls out of the station
leaving part of us on the tracks. An image
to sweeten the dusk, to mellow the lust. A couple

lulled in the ocean's trough. Nothing dramatic.
Hand holding. A scrapbook of yellowing portraits.
It's a sacred dance—her gaze locked
on mine, a steady pulse at the wrist.
My fingertips on her calves. Her belly
etched by dusky grooves that resurrect
the memory of cold delivery rooms. My bones
vibrating to her sinuous two-step. The Schumann Trio,
Maple Leaf Rag, arthritic Samba. Missteps
I've made along the way. Saddled by shame—
the orchard plundered.

I lied. I was delinquent. I was indulgent.
Clairvoyance tempers desire, holds the wisdom
of a newborn gazing into its mother's eyes—
the bond of blood.
My woman in the swimming pool. When I hold her
on my knees in the soft glow of the underwater lights,
she knows that I know for the first time,
the length and breadth. And when she pulls me to her hips,
or I trip over her ankles because she loves to dance,
I know one will fall and the other clutch at shadows.
The sostenuto of life's adagio and the hammer blows of loss
bury the floor beneath dust.

When this woman disrobes down to the holy flesh,
she gives the gift of trust, unfazed by time's jackals.

When the messenger on the freighter arrives,
clarity begins. Wellspring of sonnet and oil. One flask
poured into the other. The rightness of eyes that see.
The profligate horizon.
                        The savage letting go…

At the Funeral

nothing keener than the widow's grief
when the veteran with a lick-spittled twist
of his handle-bar mustache that flickers
like a muskrat's whiskers,
presents the flag: red for heroism;
white, purity; blue, glory,
folded like an omelet into her hands.

Taps unspools from a coronet
across the dormant orchard,
blunting the chaplain's lies
about saintliness and unswerving faith for the man
reduced to ashes in an urn
tarnished like a trophy at the widow's feet.

Back home the dog whines
in the man's empty chair, men
with grog blossoms on their noses
raise another glass of poteen
while the dead invite relatives
into yellowed scrapbooks
with *say cheese* smiles.
From that heaven beyond the pages,
they forgive the questions
that have no answers.

Time has rearranged the silver emulsion
of passing and given them repose
in the cradle of our eyes.

Dancing with Another

I have just come from a challenging
treadmill workout, looking for meditative
time in the heat, when I hear him
before I see him at the back of the room
in a thick fog of steam,

holding forth with, *Fly me to the moon,*
in a grating, baritone voice, off key.

Sinatra rolls over.

Unbidden, he is on to,
So how could I dance with another, ooh,
his voice reaching like an illness
for the falsetto, beer belly quivering
with the effort.

Lennon groans.

So, what to say—engage or suffer in silence?

Of late I am taciturn, narrow in tastes
for Bach, the Late Quartets, Elgar.

Still, his outpouring is poignant, prompts me to ask
about his love of song and achievements
in the songster realm.

He confesses there are none
beyond the shower; a tragic history of orphanage,
yearning and failure that followed.

I ask him to sing another song for me,
inviting the inevitable.

Do you like Dean? he asks.
Oh, yeah, I reply, white lie
rising like a trout to the fly.
I stiffen at the thought of that saccharine voice,
sit through, *Volare, Cantare, oh, oh, oh, oh.*

Insecurity falls away as he tightens his throat
and vocal cords, ascending to the final note.

I am weeping through a haze of steam
and eucalyptus. *Beautiful,* I say. *Simply beautiful...*

Buddha smiles.

Turning 60

One candle in a marzipan tart
burns on my 60th birthday.
My wife and daughter wait expectantly
for a wish that treads water
behind my eyes. It would be enough

to hold the fullness of this moment
that enfolds me in soft light,
to fly away now like the heron
we saw on the beach last night,
evaporate in perfect spheres

like bubbles in the champagne.
A Lionel train set sufficed
when I was a boy, could carry me off
into joy, or slap-shot from a hockey stick
or roller coaster ride. The way,
Hopkin's Windhover, does now.
Birthdays stretched ahead, an endless road
across a continent, the pure hell-bent dash
for everything. This is no easy candle
to extinguish. You blindfold me

on the way to the porch,
to the rest of my life, where
your gift of a Moon-fire maple waits.
Everything said in its rusting leaves,
the roots I will fold into autumn's bed.

Sound View

Mr. Michener dies tenaciously
    in the hospital bed. Cancer
has eaten his ears to nubs. Stroke
    has pilfered his words. Eyes
brim with the justice of hemlock.
    Right hand flails
like a netted flounder, pulls
    the nasal tube urgently
as a deacon sounds belfry chimes
    in an emergency.

He cannot see the sound view
    from the misted window,
how water spreads like curls off
    the shore's chest, blood-colored
at ebb tide, distills into sky,
    rebirths from the plump
ovulation of clouds. He is not ready
    for the legend of white light
at tunnel's end, squeezes my hand
    in search of intimacy. Eyelids
droop with the effort of not finding
    words, drool puddles on his lips.

My mumbling dissolves on muffled ears—
    how can I know this passage?
When his grandsons arrive, a half smile
    plays across slack lips, death
molds his face, placid as the sea,
    break-watered past the spit of land
known as, Point-No-Point.

Now as Then

the quiet ecstasy of night
    evaporates in animal songs,
and we desert the fragrant meadow
    for Thucydides' drumbeats.
Always one foot into the chasm,
    a dark reckoning
of baboon brains, the armada
    of wind-blown ships hard
to Sicily. This rage familiar
    as seeds to the pomegranate,
the shackles of blood. Split
    melon skulls strewn
across the moonlit fields,
    an inventory of limbs, then
as now, stacked on history's shelves
    and all those gangrenous
aspirations pollinating their fruit,
    Hellenic tears watering
the Euphrates and the small boats
    christened by Pericles' oration,
his plangent voice blown
    beneath the sun-split clouds
of the nations' darkening pall.

The Bones are Singing

At Dover Air Force Base, the Corporal
bends to his work with the focus
of a diamond cutter, drapes the bones

in the Stars & Stripes, pins the Purple Heart
to the casket's satin lining. Bleached bones
that were interred in a rice paddy,

found glinting beneath the starlight
of a summer's night, come home now after
thirty years, to a daughter not yet born,

when her father was called to war. Leg bones
that carried him into battle, arm bones
that would have cradled her, the perfect

tongue & groove joinery of his spine, scaffold
for the flesh, still straight and unyielding.
She arrives to honor him, the last and only time

she will meet her father. In what seems
an audacious act of grief, she curls her hand
around his vertebrae—adoration rising

from the macabre—begins to hum a lullaby
under her breath. Reconstructs in her imagination,
the man from these hallowed bones, the father

she knows only from yellowed photographs,
clad in camouflage, beside a helicopter. The note
found in his foot locker promising her to come home.

And everywhere, in far flung fields & forests,
beneath glaciers and deserts, ancient & contemporary,
the orphaned bones are singing…

Nautilus

Submariner
rising from the deep

into indigo waters.
Most lustrous cochlea

of hooded chambers.
Nightmares seized my child

in sleep, a black pool,
she could not escape.

Nautilus hunts on the surface,
using its parrot-like beak,

slender tentacles
writhing from their crusty purse.

Striped ambassador of the sea
contained in a ship of pearl,

buoyant as my daughter's dreams
trapped in caves of torment.

I held my child
in the throes of night terrors,

never jarred her
from the grip of the abyss,

wrapped my arms around her
as long as terror reigned.

Nautilus rises at night
when it cannot be seen,

stealthily as a submarine.
I dream of silos opening,

her small body drowning
in a blinding flash.

Relief, as we float like fish,
open-mouthed, to the surface.

When the Earth Trembles

If I ever pass this way again
I will seek you in the mountain's shadow
the lip of the ocean's wave
imperfect as we have been and this
as we came to know in time
the perfect imperfection
where sea meets land running his hand
into the fractals of her shore
through all the countries beyond
the night watch the stones pulled up by the sky
the shining roots that held your echo
and I the heron wading the shallows
waiting for a sign
when it was all there to be seen
simply by open eyes
I could have pried it from the gullet
that drop of knowledge it held
in a strand of silver minnows
the spine of our story unwound
letting the chapters flutter
in currents of pain like battered boats
drawn inland to the river's head
by the wail of an oboe's reeds soft
sound the grasses made
when the earth trembled under duress
I held on to the prow of a white morning
engraved on the estuarine flow
in the silence of animals
the sanctuary of groves
in passage comes the way

Sweetbriar

Susquehana, Mississqua;
names fragrant as eglantine
in their soft consonants—
lakes where the Chippewa paddled
through maple-leaf summers.

I joined the birch-bark boys
of Archambeault, flinty in our knees
and elbows. We ran the high grass
skipping stones, smacking the surface
like beavers, reveling in the loudest echo.

Couched in night
we rode on a silver meadow beneath
the archer's bow. Knee-deep
in the bittersweet I stand, stunned
by my aged spirit,
the mortal I have become.

A bell calls me back
to the pond's edge, to my fort in the woods
where I hear my mother's summons,
supper is ready, calls me back
to her auburn hair laced with sweetbriar,
that fragrance like the dulcet S beneath
Mississqua, Susquehana.

On a Perspective of Things

Everything hinges on belief in the invisible.
Faith follows from this. The suspension of belief
may result in obsession with only the shining surface,
and skew one's life in the mode of shallow thinking.

When the moon obscures the sun, the lovely corona
of rays that escape around the edges, that slight bend
of light proved one man's vision of time and space.

Curiosity for the hidden may seem trivial compared
to the mouth-feel of caramel chocolate, or milk
of the galaxy spread across a darkened sky. Granted,
those modest pleasures are gifts given through tongue
and eye, a foil for what lives deeper inside, if one has
temerity to gaze through a magnifying lens.

Lucretius, a visionary of audacious courage, mocked
by pagan Rome, surmised long before quantum theory,
we came from particles spawned in a time of chaos,
free will depends on the capricious swerve of atoms,
the body, the vessel that holds mind and spirit.

I am riveted by the beautiful mystery, as he was,
even as I struggle with God.

From my home, I can hear shore birds singing
from their nests on the beach, invisible waves that spiral
into my ears. And, intricate spider webs studded
with jeweled raindrops, lure winged travelers.

Most rapturous of perfections is the jiggle of atoms
through the brain, to summon your mind like a monarch,
and command your thoughts,

to secretly lift the veils.

Polysyllabic

Language is mined through my grandson's
eyes and ears—consonants and vowels
frothing on milk-flecked lips—the hard
Gs and Ks, soft Os and As assembling
like salmon at the base of a fish ladder,
in the third frontal convolution of brain.
Waiting to leap, rung-to-rung through a tangle
of pristine nerve cells quivering like tadpoles

in quiet lakes. A journey of repetition and
incubation spurred onward by perception
of line and light, circle and square, the dog
barking at the delivery van, the massage song
crooned by his mother as she strokes his limbs
with apricot oil, the crusty trill of crickets
heard from his baby rocker. All this
from one waterfall to another, ever up

to the spawning pond where fins and tails
anneal to form words fertilized in the gravel.
By nightfall, scales flash in the moonlight
linking neuron to neuron like a telegraph cable.
Even now as his lids flutter and droop, body,
heavy with sleep in my arms, the minnows
of speech prepare to rise from a shoal of babble,
netted by tongue and lips, into the light.

Crossing Over

In her white paddock,
        the woman dreams a mare,
              flanks churning

to stay afloat. Unaware
        the distance stretches too far.
              Ten to twenty knots

on the inland waves,
        but a hard wind
              fractures the surface.

Every day, shining water
        streams in rivulets
              across her back

foaming like suds,
        and the withers bunched
              in one surge

beneath all the swift torrents
        of felicity and faith,
              her mane fanned

like a wedding train
        for steerage,
              and overhead,

the relentless sun
        insolent
              to the bit,

bulging eyes, frothing lips,
        the mallard she passes,
              smoldering like an emerald

on the water's skin
        that breaks now like waves
               to drown

this struggle
        under tungsten lamps,
               the heart monitor's

vicious hum marking
        the end of her life
               in a ripple.

Faith

At last I shredded faith
and welcomed the full weight
of a cynical persuasion

relieved of invisible angels,
magisterium's holy light
and envy for devotees

mortgaged on allegory,
Eden's lascivious bite,
creation's six-day fable.

My salvation swung
on sun-split clouds,
the delicate architecture

of body and beak and all
the rowdy evidence assembled
in the courtyard that speaks

to me through whispered realms
of grace to say,
faith is the next breath.

Exhalation

       Ground greets death
in the long procession
   of brown leaves;
aspirations
       beneath our feet,
           cooked by the sun.

     Photosynthesis! I shout.
This is how we go;
   with a daub of chlorophyll
in our cheeks,
    ungloved, defatted, filleted.

     This has always been;
the horse in the ditch,
  rabbit on the road,
man in the trench,
   bone marrow blown…

We revel in the myth of flesh
      never knowing what it is,
          seduced by its turgid comfort
as it shadows these leaves
      from their green supplication
         to a spidered scaffold,

and, forever undone,
     exhales into the next thing
             we become.

The Words

If I could find the words to say my truth,
I would strew them like wildflowers

blanketing a mountainside
or hang them like prey on the spider's web

festooned with raindrops, that stretches
between the maple tree and fence post, pull

their phonemes apart to decipher the guttural
howls of my child set adrift in a skiff

beneath the glittering North Star. A few
knew I was getting lost on the ice-

packed streets as I ran with the winter boys—
some went early to the earth while the words

braided 'round my shoulders, arms and ribs,
became ropes spreading me like a trestle

between cocksure and an imbecile
impervious to mildew and shot through with it.

Light glares past a new pair of lenses
that straddle my nose like a confident lover,

that bring the words into sharp focus—
a fire scouring the forest's underbrush.

Don't tell me you understand what I'm
trying to say. Tell me. It doesn't matter.

It does. The cigar store on the corner, where
I inhaled my first Romeo & Julieta, lifted

a pack of Fleer's Double Bubble, and shot
billiards with French toughs in the back room,

left marks indelible as water stains on vellum.
Soot-stained snowbanks suffocated my youth,

bombs exploded in British mailboxes. All this
is to say something without words—

reek of cordite, the perfume of Sweetbriar
in my mother's hair. Next, came

the cloying pestilence of formalin and John Doe's
naked body cloaked in shriveled skin

on the necropsy table. Angels clamored overhead
as we peeled layers down to the darkened organs

cowering like refugees in a ship's hold. No words,
just yellowed fat on latex gloves, stink of old eggs,

and the scalpel's invasion of a foreclosed home.
The rest of this you can figure out beneath

a gunmetal sky—snow monkeys soaking in thermal
pools, a wedding of syntax to broken lines. Words

matter or they don't. The future rushed in—
a waterfall rife with jagged stones, days spent

rescuing the submerged, searching for synonyms,
and weighing the heartbeats of sentient men.

There are those scattered in the wasteland
whose bones were given to the heavy lift, ghosts

behind ancient trees feted by the sun, those who said
Kaddish for my brothers as I bent to the shovel—

flowers, hard clods of dirt raining down on coffins.
If I had the words to tell my truth, I would not say

that, "beauty is all ye need to know on earth,"
but ask in the flutter of autumn winds

what is beautiful in the maw of terror, why
leaves must, like flesh, blush and fall away.

Inviolable

We know nothing of the secret life of brain,
even as it propels ideas onto this page,

only what essence evaporates when the nectar
of blood is blocked, or parts are excised

and discarded. If we could hike its ruts and ridges,
rappel down serpiginous arteries and veins,

nothing more would we know of the 3 pound
melon floating serenely in its sterile sea.

Cut it, magnify it—the mystery deepens,
as when a fox eludes the hounds. Shock it

to elicit a twitch, lobotomize, sever
its callosal bridge. Isolated from its five senses

brain withers like corn stalks in a drought.
At autopsy, this vibrant, pulsatile organ

wears death's gray cloak. Listen to the pathologist
pontificate, measure and weigh, pluck out a tumor

that rendered this human unable to recognize
his mother's face. There's simply no way

to interrogate what cannot be seen from inside
brain's domain—no way to take a head and spin it

in a centrifuge, hoping to float nubbins of what
makes it tick. Appreciate the cortical mantle

snug as the polar ice-cap, that presses the brake pedal
to control baboon impulses waiting like lava

to overflow. At war, clad in chameleon's skin, brain
barters virtue, enables men to batter, shatter, impale

without a shudder. Where will you take us
eons from now? Will our urges be purged or must we

remain cunning as crows? We revel in high tech's
genetic code, but the secrets of cerebral splendor

stay locked in time's strongbox, inviolable
and light years remote. Everything we are, the skull

contains—forests and oceans of love and hate,
the quest to delve beyond what is said, dreams to fly

to another place. Brain, teach us to love our unlovable
selves flawed as gemstones forged in rock, forgive

the carnival masks we wear that hold our worst
nightmares of stick men, at bay. By all means,

connect the dots, probe for the seeds, chemokines,
and stars hidden in this infinite garden. Ephemera

become more opaque as answers disappear into
questions, and questions erupt

in a geyser of laughter—something cosmic
that chains us to the knowable place.

Arthur Ginsberg grew up in Montreal, Quebec where he attended McGill University medical school and trained as an internist and neurologist. A love for poetry began in his teenage years. At age 65 he earned an MFA degree in creative writing. His poems reflect a fascination with the intricacy of the brain, and devotion to humanitarian centered care for his patients. He has been blessed by a 47-year love affair with his wife, and by 2 extraordinary daughters. He received the William Stafford award in poetry in 2003 and the Humanities award from the American Academy of Neurology in 2010. His poems have appeared in such magazines as *the Atlanta Review, the Saranac Review, the Georgetown Review* and the medical anthologies, *Blood and Bone, Beyond Forgetting,* and *Primary Care.* In 2012 he began teaching a seminar on the interface between poetry and healing in the University of Washington's honors program. His collection *The Anatomist* appeared in 2013.

Also by Arthur Ginsberg

The Anatomist (2013)

Praise for *Brain Works*

"Like atmospheric rivers, we flow through each other's lives, barely aware of what blessings or trials our presence creates. And yet, sometimes we are given the privilege to enter the intimacy of another's life - as lover, as caretaker. Arthur Ginsberg, a doctor, has been such a caregiver for the greater part of his life, and he generously shares with readers through precise lyrical narratives how that dance of empathy and patience unfolds, none more moving than the nurture of his own mother. 'By candlelight, I spoon into her mouth/mamaliga, the corn gruel she loves/from Pietra Namsk in Romania,/where she grew up. What tenderness/I hold for this marred mind, how fine/to have known this palace of her spirit,/the template for mine.'"-Sandra Alcosser, *Except by Nature* and *A Fish to Feed All Hunger*

"*Brainworks* is, quite simply, a tour de force. Elegiac lyrics pair with this many-laureled physician's experience to offer nuanced insights into thought and memory. Dr. Ginsberg, a neurologist and poet based in Seattle, hones his meditations on the brain. He is not afraid to address his own mind: 'This day please be calm.' As overarching theme, the brain becomes an extended metaphor for fire: 'divine carburetion,' 'matchstick', 'sulfurous nugget.' Perhaps one of the most striking aspects is this physician-poet's ability to deconstruct the brain-to reduce its myriad operations to their constituent parts, as in 'Stroke': 'Undoing speaks to the marvel of design-/more eloquent than speech, the vespers of silence.' Ultimately, the case studies and characters that populate this book become our friends and relatives, urging us to 'ripple' with, and not against, mortality."-Judith Skillman, *Came Home to Winter*

****

Made in the USA
Columbia, SC
30 December 2019